T0147185

LITTLE BOOK OF
Hospital Miracles

LORI J. GRANDE-SWIATKOWSKI

WESTBOW
PRESS®
A DIVISION OF THOMAS NELSON
& ZONDERVAN

WestBow Press books may be ordered through booksellers or by contacting:

WestBow Press
A Division of Thomas Nelson & Zondervan
1663 Liberty Drive
Bloomington, IN 47403
www.westbowpress.com
844-714-3454

Because of the dynamic nature of the Internet, any web addresses or
links contained in this book may have changed since publication and
may no longer be valid. The views expressed in this work are solely those
of the author and do not necessarily reflect the views of the publisher,
and the publisher hereby disclaims any responsibility for them.

Any people depicted in stock imagery provided by Getty Images are
models, and such images are being used for illustrative purposes only.
Certain stock imagery © Getty Images.

Scripture texts in this work are taken from the New American Bible, revised
edition © 2010, 1991, 1986, 1970 Confraternity of Christian Doctrine,
Washington, D.C. and are used by permission of the copyright owner. All
Rights Reserved. No part of the New American Bible may be reproduced
in any form without permission in writing from the copyright owner.

ISBN: 978-1-6642-5008-6 (sc)
ISBN: 978-1-6642-5009-3 (hc)
ISBN: 978-1-6642-5007-9 (e)

Library of Congress Control Number: 2021923391

Print information available on the last page.

WestBow Press rev. date: 02/04/2022

This book is dedicated to The Lord

CONTENTS

Miracle, from the Latin *mirus*, means wonderful. The stories I have compiled are wonderful in their own way. I have been a registered nurse for over forty-two years and have taken care of thousands of people over my long career, many of whom were dying. In caring for this special group of people, I have realized that the veil between the seen and the unseen, earth and heaven, seems to be very thin. I have seen some miraculous things happen in my career (even though I did not know some were miracles at the time). I think it is important to share my story at a time when faith in God seems to be diminishing. Faith is described as a belief in something we cannot see. With an increased focus on science and proven results, we are missing the spiritual dimension of life. The spiritual side of life usually cannot be seen—I once had the privilege of seeing it—but it can be felt.

These stories attest to the fact that there is a God and that He cares deeply about all of us. He is real and works through our lives, if we only will look for His presence. Here are some of these true stories from my career. The names and some of the details have been changed to protect the privacy of my dear patients and their families. This is a message of hope.

I worked for twenty-six years in a small community hospital in Southeast Michigan, situated on the banks of the Detroit River in my hometown. The first eight years, I worked on a medical-surgical unit. We had a wide variety of patients and diagnoses. We frequently had cancer patients and other patients who had serious medical issues. We also had less seriously ill patients, who were in the hospital for some needed testing or surgery. After working on the medical-surgical unit, I worked for the next eighteen years in the nursing pool at our hospital. I was going to school to get advanced degrees and needed flexibility in my schedule and also started having my children. Being in the pool meant that I went to a different floor in the hospital each time that I worked. Some of the stories come from my nursing pool experiences.

Our system of delivering nursing care on the medical-surgical unit was called *primary care*. This meant the nurse would take care of the same patient from admission to discharge. This allowed me to really get to know my patients and their families, and they got to know me. Nurses were responsible for the patients' baths, making their beds, lifting them out of bed, administering their medications, calling the physician, and so on. We had *one* nursing assistant on the floor for forty-eight patients, so we nurses had to help each other as we provided the direct care.

This was a time when hospice did not exist. People usually stayed in the hospital until they got better or died. This meant that patients stayed in the hospital weeks or months. We developed deep relationships with our patients who were dying and with their families. We were at the bedsides of many patients who died.

1

Mamie

Mamie was a ninety-six-year-old lady from my church. She was a faithful churchgoer, and her name had been in our church bulletin for a long time in the "Pray for the Sick" section. She was a bony woman, weighing about ninety pounds, with wild-looking white hair, translucent skin, and searching, pale-blue eyes. She had congestive heart failure. Back in the '80s, we did not have the varied medicines to care for that diagnosis that we do today. We had a couple of medications: digoxin and furosemide (Lasix). Mamie, however, had been taking these medications for quite a while, and they were no longer effective. She had an oxygen cannula that was supposed to be in her nose, but it bothered her quite a bit, and she frequently took it off and wore it like a hat. This kept me busy, putting it back on. One morning, with bated breath, she said, "I want to die." I gave her a forlorn look, but she looked me in the eye and said, "I want to go home to the Lord."

"Please don't die today!" I cried.

"Nurse, I have outlived my husband and sons. All my friends are dead. No one even comes to visit me." A tear slid from the corner of her eye.

I dried her tears with a tissue and held her hand. I did not know what to say.

Mamie barely had the energy to talk to me, but she was fond of throwing her legs over the side rails of her bed and throwing herself onto the floor. She really wanted to die; she was trying to kill herself.

I felt sorry for her, but I did not know what to do for her. I tried to sit with her and hold her hand as often as I could. I would speak softly to her and pray with her. I got into trouble with my head nurse because Mamie kept "falling." I was very worried that she would injure herself seriously.

"Please don't jump out of bed anymore," I pleaded.

"I told you, Nurse; I don't want to live anymore," Mamie retorted.

I was getting frustrated because I had four other patients, and I could not stay in her room constantly to prevent her from falling (or jumping) out of bed. I hated to put a Posey vest on her, but I knew I would need to if she didn't quit jumping. (A Posey vest is a mesh vest that is used to restrain a patient to the bed. It has ties on the bottom that are secured to the bed.) It would prevent her from falling out of bed, but she might get tangled in it.

One day, as I peeked into Mamie's room, I saw her smiling and lifting her arms as she looked at the northeast corner of her room. She was barely able to speak but said, "I see the Lord."

I looked at her face, and it was transformed into a look of wonder, awe, and calm.

"Don't you see Him? He is right over there."

I looked intently at the corner but saw nothing but the television mounted on the wall. "I'm sorry. I don't see anything," I said.

She waved me away, but I suddenly had an idea—I moved the visitor's chair and her bedside table and nightstand to the other corner of the room. I moved her bed to the northeast corner of the room. She was elated! She kept looking intently in that corner and smiling. She was no longer agitated or trying to throw herself out of bed. She seemed to be talking to whomever she saw in that corner of the room.

She said, "It is the Lord. Nurse, can't you see Him now?"

I looked again in that corner but only saw the TV mounted on the wall. I looked very carefully and was hesitant to tell her again that I couldn't see Him. "No," I said sadly.

She looked disappointed in me and said, "Well, He is right there."

I kept checking on her for the rest of my shift and saw her smiling and looking radiant, gazing in the corner of that room. Mamie died that night, peacefully, in her sleep. She got her wish.

Since Mamie had such a dramatic change in her demeanor and behavior, I do believe she saw the Lord. It is not explainable by any other means.

2

Phyllis and Albert

Phyllis and Albert had been married for fifty-five years. They had been high school sweethearts and were virtually inseparable; they did everything together. Albert was my patient; he had advanced colon cancer with metastasis to his liver. He'd had a colostomy and was receiving chemotherapy.

Albert was a tall, thin man with beautiful, expressive brown eyes. He seemed to be getting thinner and weaker with every passing day. Albert had been nauseated from the chemo treatment and could not keep anything down. I was giving him Compazine, his antiemetic medication, but it was not helping much.

"Is there anything special you would like to eat?" I asked.

"I will go down to the cafeteria to get you anything you think you could eat."

"No thank you, Nurse," he said.

His wife, Phyllis, stayed with him all day and night, sleeping in the sleeper chair next to his bed. Phyllis perked up when I asked about his favorite foods, and she offered, "I will go home and make you anything you want. Is there something I can bring you that sounds good?"

He sadly shook his head. "No, nothing sounds good."

We were both crushed at this glimmer of hope that was dashed.

The colostomy was a giant problem for him. A *colostomy* is a surgical procedure in which the bowel is brought onto the abdomen and sutured onto the skin surface. The stool comes out of the bowel onto the abdomen, where we attach a bag to collect it. Not only is it a significant body-image problem, but it can also be a skin problem, as stool that contains enzymes can break down skin; the stool sits there in the bag until it's emptied. It can also be embarrassing if the stool starts to smell. Albert was vacillating between the denial and anger stages of grief and would not look at the colostomy, so I took care of it.

Optimally, the nurse teaches the patient to care for it, but when the patient will not look at it, it is hard to teach. Phyllis would watch me when I took care of Albert's colostomy, so

I taught her. (Now, remember, this was in the 1980s, when patients stayed in the hospital for weeks or months.)

Albert was not tolerating the chemotherapy very well; he was getting quite sick. He would look with sad eyes at Phyllis, who sat next to him, holding his hand. Albert knew his treatment was not working, but I knew that he was not giving up for her sake. Phyllis was getting discouraged and disappointed too in the chemotherapy.

One day, the oncologist, Dr. O., came in, looking downcast. He said that he was stopping the chemotherapy because Albert was getting too sick, and it was not working. Albert looked relieved, but Phyllis looked devastated and started sobbing.

Dr. O. held her hand and said, "I'm sorry. There is nothing else I can do."

Albert could not go home because the chemo had annihilated his white blood count. It was down to two; a normal range is five thousand to ten thousand. This was a very low white blood count. It made Albert more vulnerable to infection and unable to fight it off. Because of this, he could not have many visitors, including his beautiful young grandchildren. He missed them dearly and had pictures of them in his room. He could have no plants or fresh fruits, which he loved. (Potted plants contain dirt, and fresh fruit may contain germs that could make him sick.)

Phyllis continued to stay day and night. I ordered another food tray for her for all meals. I tried to get her the "good" coffee from the cafeteria to cheer her up, but nothing worked. She looked horrible. She said to me, "I probably smell."

I said she could take a shower in Albert's bathroom, but she refused. I begged her to go home one morning to shower and get a fresh change of clothes. "I will be here, and I will call you right away if anything changes," I assured her.

On that bright, sunny morning in May, she agreed. She left at about eight thirty. She lived only a couple of blocks from our community hospital. I went in to check on Albert at about nine o'clock. He looked so peaceful and had a smile on his face. *Wait—he looks too peaceful!* I checked his pulse and found none, and he wasn't breathing. *Oh, my goodness!* I thought. *I sent Phyllis home, and he died right after she left!*

I hoped she would forgive me. Just then, I heard my name called on the loudspeaker for a phone call. I ran out to the desk. It was Phyllis.

She said, "The clock in the house struck nine, and I heard Albert say, 'Goodbye, Phyl.' Did he die?"

I said, "That is the exact time I found him with no pulse and not breathing, so yes. I am so sorry."

"He said goodbye to me. I guess he did not want me to see him die."

"I guess not," I said.

I was stunned to know that Albert had transcended space to let Phyllis know he was going to the other side. The miracle of love!

3

Unnamed Patient

My best friend from nursing school and I had the good fortune to work with each other on the same nursing unit. One busy day, my friend asked me to peek in on her patient who had recently passed away to see if the family was there yet, as she wanted to speak with them.

When I peeked in the room, what I saw froze me in my tracks. I could not move or speak or even breathe! As I looked in on this patient, I saw a distinct golden mist, with something like gold glitter interspersed in it, hovering over the body from the head to the feet. It stayed there for what seemed like a few minutes. I kept looking, incredulous, checking to make sure I really was seeing this—and yes, I was.

As I watched with wonder, it began to rise as one unit toward the ceiling. As I saw it rise, it seemed iridescent, as the sunlight from the window was on it. It gently floated toward the ceiling and then was gone. I was awestruck. I had seen a lot of people die, but I had never seen anything like this. It was as if I was allowed to see this person's soul leave their body and go up to God. I did not tell anyone except my mom—I feared others would think I was out of my mind.

I didn't see the family come in but wish that I had. I could have told them what I'd witnessed. This would have comforted them in their time of grief.

I remembered what my mother said about my grandma. When she and Dad went to the hospital to see Grandma after she died, my mom was hesitant because my grandma had looked so bad the day before, struggling with pneumonia. When they got in her room, however, she seemed to be smiling, and there was a golden light around her.

Years later, my cousin said she saw a golden glow around my mother in her casket.

We need to remember that all people are composed of three spheres—body, mind, and spirit (or soul). I think I was shown that the soul goes somewhere to live, even though the body is dead.

4

Verna

Verna was in her late fifties. She was a very pretty lady with kind brown eyes. Her husband, Fred, came to the hospital every day and would bring her flowers from her garden. Verna had breast cancer that had metastasized to her lungs. She had done surgery and chemotherapy as treatments, but she knew she was dying.

She was a very sweet woman, always saying, "Thank you, nurses. I really appreciate all you do." She had Fred bring us some of his home-cooked food from some of her favorite recipes. When we would see Fred bringing his Crock-Pot, we knew we were in for a treat. They were such caring people.

Verna had two sons whom she said she loved dearly. One son, Brad, lived nearby and visited often. He came in after work during the afternoon shift, so I didn't get to see him, as I worked the day shift. Her other son, Tom, lived in Indiana, which was about four hours away from our Southeast Michigan location. He had a family with young children. Verna explained that they were busy with the children and couldn't get here often. I wondered if Tom knew how sick his mother really was.

One day, Verna went into a coma. Her eyes were closed, and she was unresponsive. The weird thing was that she had no blood pressure. We had every nurse on our floor come and take her blood pressure; no one could get a reading. We also called our nursing friends from other floors to try. They could not find it either. Verna's breathing was very shallow, and Fred spent a lot of time at her bedside, talking softly to her.

On Saturday afternoon, Verna's son Tom walked into her room. She'd had her eyes closed for the past three days, but when Verna heard Tom's voice, her eyes fluttered.

"Hi, Mom," he said.

Verna opened her eyes and stared at him. Tom picked up her hand and held it.

"She squeezed my hand," he said.

We were all astonished. She had been so unresponsive. Fred left the room so Tom could have some time alone with his mother. Later that afternoon, Tom came out of the room and said, "I think she stopped breathing."

We ran in to check on her and found that she had passed on. We told Tom how she had hung on, with no discernable blood pressure, for three days, waiting to see him. He broke down and cried. The power of love.

5

Delores

Delores was a pleasant Polish lady in her late seventies whom I really liked. She had bowel cancer and had two abscesses that looked like two little holes in her abdomen. A foul-smelling yellow-green drainage came out of these wounds. As part of her care, it was my job to clean, pack, and dress these wounds. I always kept the wounds clean and tried to get her up in the chair to eat her meals.

Because of the odor, I would place cups of vanilla from the hospital kitchen in the corner of her room to absorb the smell. This was before the air purifiers that we have today were available.

Her husband, Ernie, and son, Peter, would come dutifully every day. As the weeks wore on, Delores got thinner and weaker and looked very pale. The abbesses were not healing and seemed to be getting bigger. She and I both were discouraged by this.

One morning when I came in, Delores seemed happier than I had seen her in a long time.

She said, "They are coming for me."

Somewhat shocked, I asked, "What? Who?"

"My mom and dad were here last night at the foot of my bed."

I just stared at her but finally said, "Did they say anything?"

"No, they just smiled and held out their arms."

"You'd better tell your husband."

"I know."

Just like clockwork, Ernie came in her room at eleven that morning, the start of our visiting hours.

Delores said, "I have something to tell you." She repeated what she had told me, and I saw Ernie's face fall.

Ernie called his parish priest, who came right away to give her the sacrament of the Anointing of the Sick; it was very beautiful. Ernie and I held her hands during the Our Father prayer, circling her with love.

About a week later, Delores died peacefully in her sleep—with a smile on her face.

6

Mac and James

Mac was my patient. He had advanced cirrhosis of the liver from alcoholism. His belly was swollen to about the size of being ten months pregnant due to ascites (abnormal collection of fluid in the abdominal cavity). This pressure on his diaphragm made it difficult for Mac to breathe and eat. His legs looked like tree trunks, and his feet were so swollen that he could not wear shoes. He had been in and out of the hospital for about a year.

Mac had been married and had children, but he could never stop drinking and had alienated almost his entire family, including his sister. The only one who never left him was his younger brother, James, who was a couple of years younger than Mac. James came to the hospital every day and stayed many hours with his brother. He said he would drink with Mac, but it was obvious that James did not drink as much as Mac. He was a younger, healthier version of his brother.

I asked them both if Mac was on the transplant list. James shook his head slowly and told me that a person had to be alcoholic-drinks-free for one year in Michigan to get on the list, and Mac could never make it that long. James had put Mac on the list in Ohio, as there were different rules there and not so long a wait for organs. So they were very hopeful there.

"Why is the wait shorter in Ohio?" I asked.

"Ohio doesn't have a helmet law."

"Oh." It dawned on me that many healthy people died from head injuries.

Mac's doctor performed a *paracentesis* (he put a long needle in the Mac's belly and drained the fluid into bottles). We administered diuretics and albumin intravenously to get the fluid off. We worked very hard to stabilize Mac, and he finally went home with James. I prayed for him. For months, he never came back in. The nurses on the floor wondered what had happened to him.

One busy afternoon around Christmas, I looked down the hall and saw a man pushing someone in a wheelchair toward me. It was James, pushing Mac.

Mac's belly wasn't swollen, and he looked much better.

He told me he had gotten his liver from Ohio. The light was now back in his eyes, and he had a new lease on life. The love of his brother had nurtured him back to health. I told him how happy I was for him and wished him a long, happy life. The look in his eyes said it all as he squeezed my hand.

James said, "I had to come back and show you because you believed in him."

7

Dr. Fox and Celia

D r. Fox and Celia were quite a couple. He had been a prominent surgeon at our hospital; she was his lovely but eccentric wife. They had been married for over fifty years. They had no children but were very devoted to each other.

Dr. Fox had bowel cancer. His young surgeon came in and told Doctor and Missus. that he had removed all the cancer. This made us all very happy. However, it had metastasized to his liver, and that cancer was still there. Dr. Fox was becoming ever-so-slightly jaundiced. Our sweet oncologist came in and explained that Dr. Fox could have chemotherapy, but it probably would not work. Dr. Fox knew the chemotherapy would make him feel sick, so he decided not to take the chemotherapy—to Celia's dismay.

She let him know she wanted him to try it but respected his decision.

Dr. Fox started having some diarrhea and was getting weaker. Celia became more worried and frightened over the prospect of losing him. Nothing made Dr. Fox the slightest bit happy anymore. He was becoming crabby and did not want to eat much. We were very concerned about him.

Then Celia hatched a brilliant plan—she would bring him their "baby," Belle, their ten-year-old Yorkshire terrier. Of course, this was against all the hospital rules, but when Celia told me about her idea, I agreed that it might cheer him up. I was hoping that no one would find out, as I was sure to get in big trouble.

The next morning, after Dr. Fox's bath, when he was in his robe and slippers, I helped him to the chair in his room.

At almost eleven o'clock, in popped Celia with a beautiful wicker picnic basket. "I have a surprise for you, darling," she said.

"Oh, are we going to have a picnic?" Dr. Fox asked.

"No, better than that." Celia's eyes twinkled as she opened one side of the basket, and a little furry brown head popped out.

Dr. Fox immediately put his arms out, and Belle jumped into his arms. Big tears welled up in his blue eyes and fell down his face onto Belle. Celia and I had tears too. His old smile came back. At that moment, I knew I had to get him home somehow.

After that joyful visit, I called our oncologist. I explained the visit and said, "I think Dr. Fox should go home."

He agreed and started plans for discharge. (This was a big deal because we did not have hospice then.) I talked to Celia about it, and she agreed, but she was apprehensive and concerned because she could not provide all the care he needed.

We arranged for a visiting nurse, caregiver, and physical therapist to come to their house. Also, we ordered a hospital bed and some other equipment that he could have at home. Several days later, Dr. Fox went home—and was very happy to do so.

About a month later, Celia called to let us know that Dr. Fox had died peacefully in his sleep. I was very happy he had been able to go home and die there, surrounded by the love of Celia and Belle.

8

Beth Marie

Beth Marie was a little older than I was at the time—twenty-four—and she had metastatic breast cancer. She'd had a left breast mastectomy. At this time, reconstruction work was not done on breasts, so she was just missing her left breast and had a scar line on her chest. This disfigurement made her feel sad and angry. We had mostly new nurses on the floor and were all about the same age. Quite a few of us were getting married, and Beth Marie knew it. She heard us talking about wedding plans out at our nurses' station. Beth Marie came in monthly to our floor for chemotherapy, so we got to know her.

Our oncologist told Beth Marie and her mother that the chemo wasn't working, and he thought she had only several months to live. Beth Marie and her mother were understandably grief-stricken. Unfortunately, Beth Marie seemed to be stuck in the anger phase of grief.

Our chaplain, Ralph, came to see her, and she told him that she was upset that she would not have the chance to get married. She was angry that we nurses were getting married, but she was dying, so she set out to make our lives miserable. (Her plan worked—I was so miserable that at my own wedding shower, I thought of her not getting the opportunity I had.)

Beth Marie would turn her call light on constantly. She would then complain to our head nurse that we did not answer her light fast enough. When her mother came in, it was a moment of dread for us. She would march up to our nurses' station desk with a list of complaints.

Don't get me wrong—it was horribly unfair that this beautiful young lady was being denied the future life she dreamed of. We felt sorry for her and her family. It was a very difficult situation all around.

We had a staff meeting to make a special care plan for her. The nursing staff told her that a nurse would stay in her room for ten minutes if she would leave her light off for twenty minutes. I know this sounds harsh, but she would call us in to move her tissue box one inch this way or that. It was rarely anything she really needed. These kinds of actions indicated she felt a loss of control. I think she was also fearful and lonely.

We asked Chaplain Ralph for help. He began praying with Beth Marie—and something magical began happening. Beth Marie stopped putting her light on every two seconds. She wanted to get her bath done and put her best nightgown and robe on before Chaplain Ralph came in. It seemed she had something to look forward to. She now had some devotional reading on her bedside table that he had brought to her.

Beth Marie's mother asked me who left the readings. She was not pleased with my answer. She explained they were not a religious family and that they believed in scientific reasoning.

Even so, Beth Marie's personality was softening, and her anger seemed to be dissipating.

One morning, after I had received a report from the midnight shift, I looked down the hallway and saw Beth Marie's light on. I let out a sigh and walked into her room.

"Can I help you?" I asked. I looked at Beth Marie's face in the early morning April light and was surprised to see her smiling.

"I just wanted to let you know I want my bath early because today is special," she said.

I was half stunned and half trying to remember the

therapeutic communication techniques for responding properly. "Special?" I replied.

"Yes, today Chaplain Ralph is going to baptize me." You could have knocked me over with a feather! "Oh" was all I could muster to say. It hadn't occurred to me that she wasn't baptized. "Well, that's great!"

Sure enough, Chaplain Ralph came in at ten o'clock and asked me to come into the room. I asked Beth Marie for her permission to be in the room and she nodded.

Chaplain Ralph said some prayers and baptized Beth Marie, and we held hands and prayed together. I saw an ever-so-slight smile on Beth Marie's face, and her look changed for the better. Beth Marie died peacefully, a couple of weeks later, on my day off.

9

Marty

Marty was in his late twenties. He was slightly jaundiced and had spindly arms and legs and a round, swollen middle. Marty was admitted because he was getting very weak and had frequent diarrhea.

This was in the early 1980s. We had one box of latex gloves for forty-eight patients. We were taught in nursing school that wearing gloves during patient care was bad manners, so we hardly wore gloves at all.

Marty was always getting out of bed and going to the bathroom that adjoined his room. Because of his frequent diarrhea, he sometimes dripped liquid stool on the floor. Because his diarrhea was almost constant, other nurses and nursing assistants helped me with him. Before housekeeping could clean the floor, all visible body secretions or excretions had to be off the floor. So the nursing staff would wipe up the floor with paper towels before housekeeping came in.

I had to call the methadone clinic for Marty's prescription and then call the pharmacy, as Marty had a previous heroin addiction. Marty's old family doctor did not know what was wrong with him so the doctor enlisted the help of our crabbiest old surgeon. They ordered every test in the book, but each one came back negative. I know the surgeon would have loved to cut into Marty and "fix it," but he could find nothing to fix.

Marty's mother was getting increasingly frustrated. We talked, and she said she was praying to God for some answers for Marty. One day, she confronted the crabby surgeon in the hallway. "I want to know right now what is wrong with my son," she said.

"Your son does not have cancer," he bellowed.

Stunned by his vehemence, she blinked back tears. After he turned on his heel and left our floor, I went in Marty's room. Marty's mom looked me in the eyes and said, "I want Marty out of here *now*—today. I have to find out what is wrong with him."

I quickly called his old family doctor and explained what had happened. He came up to Marty's room and spoke to Marty and his mom. He wrote an order to transfer Marty to our large inner-city research hospital. I prayed that he would get some answers and help there. I packed up his belongings and said goodbye to him as the ambulance people walked him down the hall on the stretcher.

His mom said, "I will call you and let you know."

"Thanks," I said.

Exactly thirty minutes later (the time it took to get to the research hospital), I was paged to the phone. Marty had just arrived at the emergency room. My nurse friends sitting at the desk laughed, and one said, "What did you forget to send? Were all his belongings out of the room?"

I nodded and said, "I think so."

When I answered the phone, the angry emergency room nurse on the other end of the line exclaimed, "Why didn't you just tell us he has AIDS?"

Everyone sitting at the desk overheard the nurse, and they stared at each other. I nearly dropped the phone. "We didn't know," I said.

"Really?" she said in a sarcastic tone and hung up the phone.

My friends at the desk looked at me in shock. We had all taken care of him without wearing gloves for weeks. I remembered I had seen someone, somewhere, who looked like Marty, maybe on television.

Marty's mom called me and told me the news of his diagnosis. God had answered her prayer, as she now had her answer.

I called Marty's family doctor and relayed my conversation with the emergency room nurse. He was shocked also. Two days later, I received a call from Marty's mom to tell me he had passed away. I told everyone at our nurses' station. We felt so bad. That was our first experience with HIV/AIDS at our little hospital.

10

Evelyn

Evelyn was confused. That's why her sister Peggy brought her in. Evelyn was an elderly widow who was as cute as a button, but she had her days and nights mixed up. She would scream "Carol" all night—this was the name of her favorite nurse, my best friend.

Carol and I graduated from the same nursing school, so we wore the same nursing cap. We also wore our brown hair in about the same hairstyle and were also about the same height. Carol worked days, and I worked a shift of days and midnights.

During one of my shifts, at three in the morning, I tiptoed into the room after Evelyn screamed Carol's name and told her, "Carol is not here. She's home sleeping, but she will be here in the morning."

"Come here to me," Evelyn said. In the dark, I looked like Carol, and Evelyn squinted at me dark and then screamed, "You are not Carol!"

I tried to calm her down, but she screamed all the louder. This went on for weeks. Patients with rooms near hers complained; they were not getting any sleep. Of course, Evelyn slept most of the day.

On one of Carol's days off, Evelyn was my patient for the day. She started calling out, "Mora, Mora."

"Mora?" I said.

She excitedly said, "Mora was here. I saw her."

I didn't see any visitors, and her sister Peggy wasn't here yet, as it was too early for visiting hours. I asked Evelyn, "When was Mora here?"

"Last night," she stated matter-of-factly.

I was a little confused because Evelyn always called out for Carol. I didn't know who Mora was. As I saw Peggy come down the hall to visit, I walked up to her and said, "Evelyn says Mora was here last night."

Peggy's face lost its color, and she looked distressed.

"Peggy, who is Mora?" I asked.

Peggy took a deep breath and said, "Mora is Evelyn's daughter, the only child she ever had."

I thought this was strange because Evelyn had been in the hospital for weeks, and we hadn't seen a daughter visit.

Peggy whispered, "Mora died in a car accident as a very young girl."

I gasped.

"When did she say Mora was here?" Peggy asked.

"Last night," I said.

"Oh boy."

Evelyn was still sleepy but uncharacteristically quiet when Peggy was in the room.

"I heard you saw Mora," Peggy said quietly.

Evelyn looked at Peggy and said, "I want Mora."

Peggy and I were unsure of what to say next. The next night, Evelyn said she saw her dad. When I told Peggy, she said, "They are coming for her."

Sure enough, the next night, when we checked Evelyn at the three o'clock rounds, we found she had died in her sleep.

11

Harry, Tom, and Billy

Harry was my patient. He had non-Hodgkin's lymphoma that we were trying to fight with chemotherapy. From the results of the blood work and the scans, we were losing the battle.

Tom was Harry's loyal brother, with whom he lived. Harry's white blood count was so low that he was in protective isolation (now called *neutropenic precautions*); in this type of isolation, we are protecting the patient from us and our germs. Tom would dutifully "suit up" with the gown, mask, and gloves when he visited daily. He came early and stayed most of the day. Visiting hours were 11:00 a.m. to 1:00 p.m. and 5:00 p.m. to 8:00 p.m., but since the treatments were not working, Harry's doctor made an exception and let Tom stay throughout the day. (The doctor didn't know how long Harry would live.)

After making some small talk with Tom, I turned to Harry and said, "Your doctor wants to talk to you today." This was usually bad news in these situations. The doctor probably was going to suggest stopping treatment.

Harry shot a solemn gaze at Tom and said, "I want to see Billy."

"Are you sure?" Tom said quickly. "You haven't seen him in fifteen years."

I was standing in the middle of this, wondering who Billy was, but I dared not ask.

"Call him and have him come up here!" Harry shouted.

I excused myself and stepped into the hallway.

Tom came out and said, "He is dying, isn't he?"

"I think so," I said gently. "The cancer is progressing. Who is Billy?"

"He's our kid brother. There was some bad blood between them when our parents died, and their estate was split."

"Oh boy," I said.

Tom reluctantly called Billy. He went back in the room and told Harry he'd made the phone call.

The doctor came in later that afternoon, and he did suggest that we stop treatment. Harry looked relieved, but Tom looked devastated.

Several days went by, and there was no sign of Billy.

Harry's vital signs were declining, and he was semiconscious. Tom was disappointed that Billy had not come immediately. Harry was not cognizant of that fact, but I think he kept on hoping.

The next day, at lunchtime visiting hours, I saw a lone figure in the hallway, standing near Harry's door. He was reading the protective isolation sign. I went up to him and asked,

"Do you need any help?"

"Yes," he said, "my brother is in that room, and I want to see him."

I helped him put on a gown, mask, and gloves, and he went in the room. Shortly afterward, when I went in the room to administer Harry's noon medications, I found both men crying—a mixture of sad and happy tears. It was a strange coincidence—or maybe not—that Tom was not there. I think his absence was meant to be so that these two brothers could reconcile and make peace.

Billy stayed for about an hour. After he left, Harry said to me, "I am so glad I got to see my kid brother. I never thought I would see him again. Thank you if you helped in any way to make this possible."

"Tom is the one who called him," I said. "I didn't really have much to do with it."

Harry smiled and said, "Thank you anyway."

When the midnight nurse came in that evening, she found Harry had died, but he had a smile on his face.

I have included this story—and I have experienced many others like it—because in the 1990's, the assisted suicide movement came to light. The thought was that it was better for people with terminal illnesses to be able to end their lives. I have seen many deathbed reconciliations in my time at the hospital. I do believe there is God's timing that allows people to be brought together. Hard hearts need time to soften. It is God's timing and plan that make these miracles possible. When we humans rush things, we lose the opportunity for God to make things right.

12

John Pope

J ohn Pope was an elderly man with big blue eyes and dark brown hair. He had a very elderly wife, who was very tiny with white hair. He came into the hospital looking very frail. He had heart disease and found it difficult to breathe. He was six feet tall and weighed maybe 150 pounds. His wife had visual difficulties and could not drive.

They were very religious people. John always held his rosary, and his mouth moved in silent prayer. He also wore a brown scapular. The original brown scapular was given to Saint Simon Stock by Our Lady of Mount Carmel. (The promise is if you die while wearing the scapular, you will escape the fires of hell.)

John talked to me about his love for Jesus. He cried

when he talked to me about Jesus's crucifixion and suffering on Good Friday. He felt so bad that Jesus had to suffer for our sins. I was taken aback by his strong emotion when he spoke of Good Friday. I had never seen someone cry over the passion and sufferings of Jesus. I got the feeling that he was very close to Jesus and maybe he felt some of Jesus's sufferings.

His daughter brought his wife to see him. They exchanged a very sweet display of affection. She sat next to his bed and held his hand for quite a long time. He had difficulty speaking because he had difficulty breathing, so he didn't say much. His daughter Celeste was very active in the Blue Army and asked me to attend a First Friday mass with her, which I later did. The Blue Army is a group dedicated to spreading the message of our Blessed Mother at Fatima. Her message there (in a nutshell) was to pray the rosary, pray for the conversion of sinners, and make reparations for sin. John's entire family was very religious and were believers in Jesus Christ.

John was in the hospital for about a week when his condition took a turn for the worse. I called his daughter and asked her to bring his wife to the hospital. Celeste asked me to call for the priest, so I did. He gave John the sacrament of the Anointing of the Sick and prayed with John.

John stopped breathing at three o'clock on Friday, with his wife and daughter at his bedside. I thought how fitting it was that he died on Friday at 3:00 p.m., as he often talked about Good Friday and Jesus suffering on the cross, and this is the time we believed Jesus died. His family understood that too. John's wife, daughter and I looked at each other with unspoken words and knew it was a sign that Jesus took John to heaven on that day.

Note: The day that I was working on writing John's story, I randomly opened my Bible for guidance. The page to which it opened had the holy card (memorial prayer card) for John in it. I hadn't seen that holy card for many years. I took that as a definite sign that God wanted John's story to be told.

13

Sadie

One of my longtime and best nursing friends had nursing students in a nursing home, and she told me the following story:

Sadie was the oldest person living in the nursing home; she was 112 years old.

The residents and staff all loved her. She had been very active at the nursing home for many years, as she had her mental faculties about her. She cared for others and showed her compassion and kindness in many ways. One morning, when my friend brought the nursing students to the nursing home, she knew the atmosphere was different. It seemed very quiet, calm, and reverent. She found out that the night before, Sadie had died.

Sadie had been telling other residents that she was seeing angels in the building. And before she died, she said her room was full of angels, and they were surrounding her.

There was such a sense of peace in her room that the staff believed her.

14

Beverly

Beverly was a beautiful retired nurse who previously had worked at our hospital. She looked in very good physical shape, except she had the diagnosis of colon cancer, and it had metastasized to her liver.

She had a colectomy with a resection of her colon. This meant she had a large incision on her abdomen that I would clean and dress every day. The surgeon who performed her operation was one of our oldest and crabbiest surgeons. Dr. Crabby and Beverly had worked together for many years and had become friends.

Beverly was distraught over her cancer diagnosis. She had retired not long ago, and she had plans to travel and enjoy life with her doting husband. She was weak from the surgery and was trying to walk and get her strength back. She was very discouraged about her slow progress. Her dear husband came in every day and tried to encourage her.

Our oncologist had talked to her about chemotherapy and the chances that it would work.

She told me, "I don't like the odds of it working. I want to try something else, but I'm afraid to tell Dr. Crabby because I value his friendship. I'm worried about what he will think of me."

I talked to her and told her to pray about it. So she did.

After a few days, Beverly and her husband asked for a meeting with Dr. Crabby and Dr. O., our oncologist. I also was in the room for the meeting. I had no idea what Beverly and her husband wanted to say.

Beverly's husband thanked both doctors and asked them to discharge her. He and Beverly had done some research and wanted to go to Mexico for Laetrile treatments. He explained that Laetrile was made from apricot pits and was all natural, as opposed to the chemical chemotherapy.

Both Dr. Crabby and Dr. O. tried to talk them out of it, saying there was no scientific evidence that it actually worked. Beverly and her husband stayed firm on their decision, and in the end, the doctors agreed to discharge her the next day.

The next morning, when I was helping Beverly to get dressed and packing up her belongings to go home, Dr. Crabby came in to see her. He told her he did not agree with her decision, but he respected it. He gave her a hug and wished her well. He told her to call his office when she got home.

When he left the room, she looked up at me and thanked me.

"For what?" I asked.

"For believing in me and helping me to pray about this," she said. "I did not want to lose my friend Dr. Crabby."

"You didn't lose him," I said.

I was happy to support Beverly and her husband in their decision, even though my own feelings on the matter were unsure.

I do not know if Beverly went to Mexico for treatment. We never heard from her again.

15

Theresa

Theresa was a lady from my church who was in her early sixties. She had brown hair and kind brown eyes. Theresa was married and had two adult children. She also had kidney failure. She was on the renal diet and fluid restriction, but it was not working. She was retaining fluid and getting quite edematous (swollen). I could tell that Theresa's attentive husband was very worried. Her family doctor suggested she get on the list for dialysis.

In the early 1980s in Southeastern Michigan, there were only a few dialysis machines. There were about five in Ann Arbor at the University of Michigan Hospital, about forty-five minutes from our town. Those who needed dialysis were put on the wait list. Very frequently, people died before they got to the top of the list to receive dialysis. Theresa knew it was a long shot that she would live to receive dialysis. She asked all of us to pray for a miracle—that she would be able to have dialysis. And pray we did. She also asked her church family to pray.

About a month later, we found out that Theresa somehow had made it to the top of the list and was receiving dialysis. She also was found to be a candidate for a kidney transplant and was on the transplant list. It was more than we had hoped for. God is rich and generous! We knew it was quite a miracle.

16

The Ghost on Cardiac Care

One afternoon shift, I was working on the cardiac care unit of our hospital. I was in the back hall, which means I had four patients who were recovering from myocardial infarction (heart attack) or heart failure. The afternoon shift started at three o'clock and ended at eleven thirty at night. It was a busy night, with patients and visitors walking around. Toward the end of the shift, the nurses turned off the overhead lights in the hallway to help the patients get ready for bed and sleep.

I was walking down the darkened hallway when I saw a lady in a pink bathrobe, walking toward the solarium (a sitting room at the end of the hallway). I thought this was strange because the lights were out in that room. As I turned to get a better look at her, she started disappearing, as if an eraser started from her feet and went to the top of her head. I stood there, staring at her disappearing form, and then quickly walked back to the front desk. I told the nurses at the desk that I'd seen someone disappearing in the hallway. They did not seem surprised. One said, "Oh you saw her? We see her now and then."

I was shocked to hear this but then thought of all the patients who had died there over the years, and it made sense.

17

Radiation Shrank the Tumor

My patient Sally had a cancerous tumor in her brain. She did not want brain surgery, opting instead for radiation therapy. She and her family were praying to Jesus for a healing miracle. Because we didn't have radiation therapy equipment at our small hospital, Sally went by ambulance to another hospital for her treatments every afternoon.

She'd been hospitalized because she was having double vision and coordination problems, including problems with her balance we were afraid she would fall. (This was long ago, when people were even hospitalized for tests.)

After some time, I noticed that Sally was regaining her coordination, ever so slightly. She could feed herself and did not seem as unsteady on her feet. After about a month of treatments, Dr. O., our oncologist, ordered a CT scan of her head.

Later, he came on the floor, smiling a very big smile. We wondered what was up because he rarely treated us to that smile. He had a large manila envelope in his hand with Sally's CT scan pictures. He proudly proclaimed, "It's working!"

"What's working?" I asked.

He showed us Sally's previous CT scan and her new CT scan, and the tumor was noticeably shrinking—it was quite a bit smaller.

Sally and her family were elated! The power of prayer was very evident.

Sally went home and continued her treatments until the tumor was no more. She and her family got their miracle.

18

Robert and the Brain Tumor

In the early 1980s, I had a patient named Robert, who was in his late forties. He had a beautiful wife and three beautiful school-aged children. He was admitted to the hospital because he was having excruciating headaches.

The CT scan showed a brain tumor in the frontal area of his brain. Our neurosurgeon recommended surgical removal of the tumor, followed up with radiation. Robert was apprehensive (and rightly so) about the operation. He talked it over with his wife and children, and they decided to do the surgery. Robert explained that he wanted the cancer out of his body, as he wanted to live and be with his family.

Robert and his wife were faithful churchgoers and had a

lively faith. Their minister came to the hospital and prayed with them. Friends from their church also came to pray.

Right before Robert went to surgery, he told me he was afraid he would never wake up.

I was alarmed at his statement. "You still can cancel the surgery," I told him. "We could call your doctor right now."

He declined, saying, "I've already decided to go through with it."

Robert survived the surgery, but he didn't regain consciousness—to everyone's dismay. Robert's wife came every day to talk to him and pray for him. It was heartbreaking to see her with him.

She told me Robert loved rainbows. He said they were a bridge to heaven. One afternoon, we had a sudden rainstorm when the sun was out. A beautiful rainbow appeared over the river outside his hospital window. It was at this time that Robert took his last breath—a sign from heaven.

19

Walter and Estelle

Walter was a wonderful man in his late sixties who was
admitted to the hospital for multiple myeloma. (This is a
cancer that attacks the bone marrow.) His wife of fifty years,
Estelle, was a pretty woman with brown hair and dancing
hazel eyes. She came every day and smiled at him while she
held his hand. Walter's son was our new pharmacist, Eric,
who was engaged to our cute physical therapist Annie.

Walter came in each month for chemotherapy treatments
to combat his multiple myeloma.

Eric and Annie's wedding was approaching, but Walter's
white blood count had gone down quite far, and Dr. O., his
oncologist, advised Walter not to attend the wedding. This
was devastating to Walter and Estelle because Eric was their

only child. Dr. O. was concerned, however, because the wedding was a large one, with two hundred guests invited. He explained that Walter's immune system was compromised because the chemotherapy had stunned the bone marrow; this meant Walter's bone marrow was not producing many white blood cells. Dr. O. explained that Walter would be susceptible to any germs the guests had and could develop a serious illness that he would not be able to fight off.

Walter and Estelle were very upset about the possibility of not attending Eric's wedding. Annie and Eric had been dating for a long time, and they already thought of Annie as a daughter and were looking forward to the wedding.

They asked the nurses to pray that they would be able to attend the wedding. We started praying. We also started giving Walter a medication that would stimulate his bone marrow to make white blood cells.

Eric would come up from the pharmacy for a visit with his father and the nurses. He told us he was concerned about his dad and didn't want anything to happen to him. We only had a couple of weeks to get Walter in shape to attend the wedding—it was a race against time. Every day, we held our collective breath when the blood-work results came back. And every day, Walter's white blood count came back a little higher!

It finally was the day before the wedding. Dr. O. agreed

to let Walter attend the wedding if he promised to wear a mask the entire time. Walter promised to do just that.

The next month, when Walter came back for his chemotherapy, he had a huge smile on his face. He brought a small photo album of wedding pictures, showing him in his mask with Estelle at his side at Eric's wedding. It was wonderful to see!

Normal white blood cell counts are five thousand to ten thousand, and Walter's white blood count was only at two when we started trying to boost it up. This was a miracle!

20

Jo Marie

Jo Marie was a beautiful twenty-year-old girl with golden curls who happened to be a type one diabetic and born blind. She was faith-filled and gracious, even though she was very ill with brittle diabetes. *Brittle diabetes* means that it was very hard to get her blood sugar regulated. It was four hundred one time and sixty the next. (Normal fasting blood sugar, or glucose, levels are seventy to one hundred.)

She had to get her fingers poked before each meal and at bedtime to find out her blood sugar/glucose number, and she was getting tired of it. Her fingers were bruised and very sore. (This was in the early 1980s, when we didn't have any other method of getting a reading, such as Dexcom meters or insulin pump.)

Over the weeks, we developed a wonderful therapeutic relationship. Jo Marie's mother, Mary, came in each morning at eleven o'clock for visiting hours, and we would talk. At that time, I was about to get married, and we talked about my wedding plans. Both Jo Marie and her mother were very interested and excited for me.

Mary helped Jo Marie with her lunch. Since Jo Marie was blind, her mother arranged her tray like the face of a clock so Jo Marie would know where everything was. Mary placed Jo Marie's milk at twelve o'clock, her soup at three o'clock, her sandwich at six o'clock and her Jell-O at nine o'clock.

Jo Marie's health was not improving, and she was getting discouraged. I asked if she would like to talk to our hospital chaplain. She readily agreed, and he came in that afternoon. He talked and prayed with Jo Marie, and she became calmer.

Jo Marie's doctor came in and wanted to try a new schedule for her insulin. Within a few days, Jo Marie's blood sugar/glucose was regulated. She said it seemed like a miracle!

About a month later, I got married, and Jo Marie and her mother Mary surprised me by attending my wedding. It was so special and wonderful to see them sitting in the church! It was truly a gift and blessing for which I was thankful.

21

Angel

Angel was my patient who had wild black hair, beautiful chocolate eyes—and a groin abscess from shooting up heroin. This wound had to be cleansed and packed with Nu Gauze every twelve hours. (Nu Gauze is a sterile ribbon-like piece of gauze.) The wound was quite deep, and its location was very embarrassing for Angel.

Angel was very quiet and shy. She did not speak much when I first met her. She was frightened and ashamed of how she got her wound. I knew by looking in her eyes that she could feel the disgust and contempt of some of her caregivers. I felt the sadness this caused her.

Because of the reason for the abscess, some of the doctors and nurses were not very kind to Angel. They would mutter at the desk that she had done it to herself. I was very sad to hear this, as addiction is a disease. I wondered how they had forgotten this. Weren't they taught this in school? She did not choose this. Where was the compassion for her?

As time went by, Angel became more withdrawn and sadder. I wanted to make her feel better and show her someone cared. I noticed her hair needed a shampoo, so I got the bedfast rinser. (This is a tray you put on the bed so you can wash the patient's hair while she's lying in bed, pouring water from a pitcher onto the hair. The water drains from the tray into a bucket on the floor.)

I washed Angel's hair and combed it out for her.

She was so appreciative. "No one has ever done that for me," she told me.

"I would want someone to do that for me," I said.

She just smiled as she looked at herself in the mirror.

Knowing that people have three spheres—body, mind, and spirit—I began thinking of the root cause of Angel's illness. Her body was otherwise healthy, and she did not seem to have a mental illness. I wondered if this had a spiritual origin. I began praying for Angel.

One afternoon, I asked Angel, "Do you believe in God?"

"Of course, I do" she said.

"God sent His only son, Jesus to save us and Jesus loves you."

Angel began to cry. "I have done a lot of bad things in my life. How could Jesus love me?"

"He loves you anyway" I said.

I called our hospital chaplain to come to see her. He came to pray with her, and she seemed to get healing in the spiritual realm.

As Plato said, "So neither ought you attempt to cure the body without the soul; and this is why the cure of many diseases is unknown to the physicians, because they are ignorant of the whole, which ought to be studied also; for the part can never be well unless the whole is well."

I began to see a series of slight changes in Angel. She began to smile more. She was asking for things that she needed. Angel was speaking more and making more eye contact. She had more confidence. She was eating her protein foods, and her wound was no longer as deep; it was healing.

Her doctors determined that her infection was gone, and she could be discharged. We made discharge arrangements to send her to her friends' home, with a visiting nurse to help with the dressing changes. She also had appointments set up with her substance abuse counselor and her doctor. Angel was very appreciative and happy to be leaving the hospital. I was happy for her too. I hoped and prayed that she would stay away from the drugs.

About a month later, I received a thank-you card from Angel. It was beautiful. She wrote many things on both the front and the back of the card. The thing that stood out most of all was this: "You were the only person that treated me like a human being."

I cried, and I thought of the phrase, "Everyone is made in the image and likeness of God," as well as the Golden Rule: "Do to others what you would have them do to you" (Matthew 7:12). Everyone deserves care and respect.

I still have Angel's card tucked in my Bible, and I pray she is doing well.

22

The Angry Patient

I was in the nursing pool, which meant that I made my own work schedule. This was important when I was going to school and, later, when I had my children. When I went into work, I had to check in with the nursing staffing secretary, and she would tell me which floor to work on. I might be sent to almost any floor in the hospital. On one afternoon shift (3:00 p.m. to 11:30 p.m.), I was sent to the cardiac care unit. Because I was a pool nurse, I was sometimes given the "tough" assignments—the ones the other nurses did not want.

I was told one of my patients was a challenge. The rest of the nurses were smirking, and the nurse who reported off to me said of the patient, "She was on her call light all day, very angry, just wanting to go home." The day-shift staff had been answering this call light from the intercom at the front desk without going in the room. They told me the patient became more insistent as the day wore on.

As I was getting my report from the day shift nurse, I looked down the hallway and saw that her call light was on. I sighed and thought, *It's going to be a long night.*

Instead of ignoring this lady, I made the decision to find out what was going on. I went into her room and introduced myself. I sat down near her bed and asked, "How can I help?"

"I was admitted for a possible heart attack, but that was ruled out." This was good news! "But I still have lingering chest pain, and my doctor is trying to figure it out. It's very important that I am home this afternoon. I begged the day-shift nurses to call my doctor to release me, but they refused. They said he would come in after office hours. They also pointed out that I'm still having some chest pain." I had walked in her room at 3:45 p.m., so she was very upset, as it was getting late. "Could you call my doctor?"

"Sure," I said.

She looked me in the eye as she said, "Today is a very important day for me. I didn't want to tell the other nurses because they were so snotty to me. My son gets out of prison today. I wanted to be in the house when he comes home. He has been gone for seven years, and I haven't seen him in a long time."

I was shocked to hear this and was filled with understanding. I called her doctor from her room and told him, "She wants to be discharged today because her son is coming home."

"I knew about this," he said, "but I didn't know the exact day." He immediately discharged her, with the instructions to call his office for an appointment.

I helped her to get dressed, and a family member came to get her. She thanked me profusely, and I almost cried in front of her.

This patient taught me that you never know what people are dealing with. As my mother used to say, "Put yourself in their shoes." It's important to have kindness, compassion, and really listen.

23

Ivy

I walked in the darkened room at 7:30 a.m. to assess my new patient. Ivy was a spry, petite, eighty-year-old lady with large, expressive hazel eyes, who did not look her age. She had brown hair and not many wrinkles.

She had a large dressing on her left shoulder, and her left arm was in a navy-blue sling. When I introduced myself, she barely made eye contact with me.

It was two weeks before Christmas, and snowflakes were falling softly outside her window. Ivy had a broken left shoulder and had had shoulder surgery. She explained that she had been walking to the mailbox to mail Christmas cards, and as she was crossing the street, she got hit by a Ram pickup truck. I was perplexed why her shoulder was broken and not her leg or hip.

"I have so much to prepare before Christmas," she said, clearly very upset. "I don't have time to be laid up."

I didn't know what to say, as I knew she would be not able to use that shoulder or arm for quite some time. She would need weeks of physical therapy too.

She did not want to eat. She just wanted to sleep. I thought, *She deserves a break, She just went through a big surgery.* Even so, I wasn't sure if she was going into depression or if she was just tired from surgery.

At lunchtime, her son Buck came in. He grabbed her right foot and playfully tugged on it, saying, "Ma, wake up."

She woke up and gave the tiniest of smiles. "Oh Buck, it's you."

I told Buck that his mother did not want to eat or do anything. I explained that her sadness regarding her injury could lead to depression.

He looked very concerned and asked me to step out into the hallway with him. "My mother is very independent and the matriarch of the family," he told me. "She does a lot for everyone, including her church. Her being injured and not being able to help others and prepare for Christmas—her favorite holiday—means depression is a possibility. I'll think of something."

The next morning when I greeted Ivy, I found her more withdrawn and sadder.

She said, "Nurse, I can only move my fingers on my left hand, and I can't move my arm at all."

"Movement will come back slowly," I explained. "You'll need physical and occupational therapy to regain full function of your arm and hand."

"How long will that take?"

I replied honestly, "I don't know. We will ask your doctor today."

She just nodded and gave me a sullen look.

I helped her with her breakfast and her bath. At 11:00 a.m., the start of visiting hours, Buck came in, smiling and holding a big bag. I wondered what he had in there. He said, "Ma, I brought you something."

Ivy looked up and watched him take out a Santa Claus figure dressed in red velvet; it was over a foot tall.

"Wow!" I said.

"That isn't all—look, Ma," Buck said. He pressed the right foot of the Santa, and it began dancing and singing, "Grandma Got Run Over by a Reindeer." It was hilarious!

Ivy's hazel eyes twinkled, and she laughed. "Oh Buck, where did you find this?"

"Never mind," he said. "Nurse, I want you to show all the nurses, doctors, and therapists this. Just push the button on his right foot."

"I will," I said.

Ivy's room became a fun place for us to be. I would tease her and tell her it was the party room. I showed all my colleagues the dancing Santa, and Ivy would smile. She got to know all the workers on our floor. She began to talk and smile more and participate more in her therapy. Her spirits were lifting.

Soon, it was time for Buck to take her home with her dancing Santa. It was so wonderful to see humor help to heal her.

As I walked out to the parking lot after work, a Ram pickup truck happened to be parked near my car. I walked up to it and noticed the hood was even with my shoulder. The mystery of why Ivy had a broken shoulder was solved.

24

Bed Facing East

Fatima was a beautiful sixty-year-old Muslim woman who was admitted for a heart condition. Fatima was very weak and needed her medications regulated. She was a very religious woman and prayed several times a day. She was interrupted, however, by doctors, nurses, nursing assistants, and therapists every time she wanted to pray. She was very upset about this and said this was a reason she was not getting better.

Her family came in each day at visiting hours and read favorite prayers to her. She still was not happy. She told me, "I would pray facing the east at home, and it gave me a sense of peace."

That got me thinking. Maybe I could place her chair

facing east—but she was still very weak and could not sit up very long. I then got the idea to move her bed at an angle so it was facing east. "Here we go," I said as I pushed her bed into position.

This pleased her very much! I also put a DO NOT DISTURB sign on her door when she wanted her prayer time. A sense of peace and calm came over Fatima and her family too. Soon after that, she started getting better and was able to be discharged home.

On her day of discharge, she held my hands, looked at me, and said, "Thank you."

I was so happy I could help her. I do believe that by nurturing her spiritual realm, her physical realm responded with speedy healing.

25

The Baby

My patient Elsie was a beautiful ninety-year-old with chronic lung disease. In the morning when I would wake her, she sometimes had her oxygen cannula on the top of her head instead of in her nose. Because of this and various other reasons, she was not improving very quickly, and she was getting disappointed.

With chronic illnesses, there's a danger that the patient will feels powerless and then fall into hopelessness. Hopelessness often leads to death.

I noticed Elsie had a little Bible in her purse, so I asked her if she wanted our chaplain to visit, and she said yes. Our hospital chaplain was a very kind man who visited and prayed with Elsie every day. She slowly started to get better and stronger.

One pretty morning, as the sun was coming up over the river, she said to me, "Today is a special day."

"Why?" I asked.

"Nurse, my baby is coming to visit me today."

"Wow," I said. I was excited because we didn't get many children visiting on the floor. And to see a baby—well, that was special! I did think of the hospital rule that said children had to be twelve years or older to visit, but Elsie seemed so happy and excited. I didn't want to tell her that rule and burst her bubble. Besides, I wanted to see the baby too.

Elsie wanted her bath early, and she wanted to put on her own pretty nightgown and robe. I helped her with her bath, combed out her hair, and got her dressed in her own nightgown and robe. She wanted to sit in the chair too, so I helped her up and sat her in the chair. It was lunchtime, and several nurses were at lunch, so it was quite busy for those of us who were still there. I was running around, answering call lights, and trying to give my own patients their noon medications. I was so busy that I forgot about the baby.

A while later, I peeked into Elsie's room and saw a little bald man sitting next to her chair, holding her hand. I wondered where the baby was.

Elsie saw me and said, "Nurse, come here. I want you to meet my baby."

You could have knocked me over with a feather! I was surprised that this older gentleman was her "baby"! It did come to mind that Elsie was ninety years old. It then made sense that her baby would be in his late sixties or even seventy. Her son's bald head and face got flushed when she called him her baby.

"Oh, she always calls me that," he said when he saw the surprise register on my face.

"Well, she did say her baby was coming" I said.

"I am the youngest," he said.

In the scheme of eternity, he certainly was a baby. Thinking about it later, I guessed it was all relative to each person's perception.

Elsie's baby son said he was taking her home with him when she got discharged. I saw the look of love in her eyes, and she had hope for the future. She started getting better quickly and was discharged soon after.

26

Clara and Howard

Clara was a beautiful Polish woman who had been married to her devoted husband, Howard, for forty-five years. They had no children but had nephews who were close to them. Clara had a heart problem that was misdiagnosed for years. (Years ago, women were often told they had anxiety or depression issues instead of cardiac issues.) She was given tranquilizers and other antianxiety medications to treat her very unstable angina. She threw those away and finally got a new physician, who gave her nitroglycerine, which sometimes helped.

Clara struggled with her cardiac illness for a long time. I took care of Clara on the cardiac care unit. One night, Clara had a cardiac arrest, cardiopulmonary resuscitation (CPR) was performed, and her heart started beating again.

Later, Clara said, "Nurse, during the time my heart stopped, I felt like I was outside my body on the ceiling. I was watching the nurses and doctors working on me." I just looked at her and nodded.

"I traveled in a tunnel and then saw a light and was in heaven with Jesus. All my pain was gone."

"That must have been wonderful," I said.

"Heaven was so beautiful Nurse. I saw colors so vibrant and different from earth. I was so disappointed when I came back into my body."

"You were disappointed," I reiterated.

Clara nodded and said, "All of the good feelings were gone, and I was back in pain."

Howard came in at eleven the next morning for visiting hours.

Clara told him all about her experience in heaven. "I didn't want to come back here!" she said.

Howard was quite upset and hurt. He said, "You didn't want to come back to me?"

"No, I'm sorry. I did not. In fact, I want to go back!"

Howard was crestfallen, as he and his wife were so close. "Well, I'm still happy that they brought you back to me," he said.

Clara did not say anything.

As Howard sat looking at her, I could see he was wondering when she would leave him again for good.

Several months later, Clara's doctor told us she died at home, peacefully, in her sleep.

27

Eleanor

Eleanor was in her mid-eighties. She was a tiny, independent woman with white wild hair, translucent skin, and expressive blue eyes. She'd had bowel obstruction surgery two weeks earlier and now had pneumonia. Eleanor was very discouraged by this, as she wanted to get home, pronto.

The other problem was that her pneumonia was not getting any better. (In those days, pneumonia patients had a chest x-ray every day.) Her white blood count was not coming down either, which was a sign that her infection was not going away. Her doctor was stumped and added a very powerful intravenous antibiotic to her other antibiotic regimen.

Eleanor asked, "Nurse, do you believe in angels?"

"Of course," I replied.

Her eyes twinkled. "I am going to pray for my guardian angel to watch over me and ask Jesus to heal me."

"Good idea."

When I came back the next morning, Eleanor was excited to tell me she'd seen her guardian angel the previous night.

"Wow," I said as I looked at her incredulously.

"He stood at the foot of my bed," she said.

"What did your angel look like?"

"He was very tall and big," she said.

I asked, "How tall?"

She pointed upward. "He was as tall as the ceiling."

I was surprised to think that her angel was that big, as I had thought of little cherubic angels with wings. "Did he say anything?" I asked.

"No, he just smiled."

This reminded me of the Bible verse, "For my angel is with you, and he will keep watch over you" (Baruch 6:6).

Miraculously, Eleanor's chest x-ray that day showed much improvement. Within a couple of days, Eleanor was discharged home, with a visiting nurse consultation. Her guardian angel had let her know that her prayer was heard, and that Jesus was healing her.

28

Parking Lot Stranger

It was a very busy night, and I was working late on the afternoon shift; it was now midnight. All the other afternoon-shift workers had left at 11:30 p.m. This meant I would be walking out to the parking lot alone. I usually waited for security to take me out to my car, which was parked far away from the hospital in the employee lot. On this night, I debated whether I should wait for security to pick me up at the front door. Even though it would be much safer to wait for security, I was very tired and just wanted to get home.

I ventured out into the blustery Michigan spring night. As soon as I stepped out of the door, a man came out of the other front door. I looked back at him. He was about thirty feet from me. *He's a visitor going out to his car,* I thought. It was very windy that night, and the wind was pushing me back. I suddenly noticed the man was gaining on me and seemed to be coming after me. How foolish I had been, not to wait for security. My car was far out in the darkened parking lot by itself. There was no one around to help me. Even if I screamed, no one would hear me. I prayed, "God change his mind. Please change his mind about coming after me." I kept repeating this prayer. My adrenaline was going full blast, and I started running to my car.

Suddenly, I saw the man turn on his heel and stop chasing me. "Thank you, God, for changing his mind," I said.

I practically fell into my car and locked the doors, still shaking. I never did that again.

Give thanks to the Lord for He is good, for his mercy endures forever. (Psalm 118:1)

AFTERWORD

I hope you have enjoyed these true stories from my career. The Lord has wanted me to share these stories for quite some time now, so I apologize for not sharing sooner. I have been busy with my teaching career and was not able to devote the time to my story. My recent retirement gave me the time and energy to complete this; it has been many years in the making.

My own Catholic faith has played a role in my spiritual development. I have known since I was a young child that God exists, and there is a supernatural realm where things happen and an afterlife where our souls/spirits go.

My nursing career of forty-two years (and three science degrees) have put me squarely in the world of science. The disciplines of nursing and medicine are rooted in science. Science is grounded in data and results of the physical world. The scientific method consists of a hypothesis, experimentation, and analysis of results. By the laws of probability, the same results should come from the same experiment. But sometimes, things happen that defy science. They don't have a logical explanation.

The fact is that the spiritual realm is much larger than the physical one. Just because we cannot see it doesn't mean it does not exist. It can be felt with the heart. The power of prayer is real. It changes things. I have seen it happen!

Faith needs to be strengthened, and hope needs to be nurtured. God needs to be relevant. He exists in the supernatural and natural. He is real! We only need to open "the eyes of our heart" (Ephesians 1:18) to see Him.

He will help us, if we call upon Him. He is working silent miracles every day, if we would only look and listen. Remember that the Lord was not heard in the wind but in the gentle whisper (1 Kings 19:11–13). Let us be alert and not asleep to recognize the presence of the Lord.

Look for the little miracles in your life. I'll bet you will find them and find a wonderful, loving God who is making them happen.

ACKNOWLEDGEMENTS

- I would like to thank all my encouraging friends especially, Carolyn, Marsha, Denise, Denise, Renee, Jill, Yasuko and Karen who gave me Sadie's story.

- A big thank you to Peggy for graciously being my sounding board, thesaurus and using your computer savvy to help me with social media.

- Thank you to my niece Lindsay and sister Lynn for proofreading and helping with my photo.

- Thank you to Joe, Danielle, Bob, Kelly, my editor Marva and all my friends at Westbow Press who helped to make my dream a reality.

- Many thanks to Ruth Olson Photography for my author photo.

- Thank you to my dear husband Ken, sons Timothy, Nicholas, Jonathon and brother John for your constant love and support.

- Thank you Mom and Dad for your endless love.

- I can't forget to thank God for everything.

Printed in the United States
by Baker & Taylor Publisher Services